VIGILANTE FOR JESUS

VIGILANTE FOR JESUS

Katherine Michelle Woods

Kawoo Book Publishing
Chicago, Illinois

VIGILANTE FOR JESUS
Published by
Kawoo Book Publishing
Chicago, Illinois
kawoo30645@yahoo.com

Katherine Michelle Woods, Publisher / Editorial Director
Yvonne Rose/QualityPress.info, Book Packager

ACKNOWLEDGEMENTS

I especially want to thank my daughter, Dr. Susan Gaffney and my brother, Michael Griffin, for their editing assistance, and Marc Moran for providing the graphics. May God bless you and keep you. I pray you will enjoy my book.

CONTENTS

PREFACE

My name is Vince Jones; however, when someone asks me my name, I say V J. My initials, V J stands for Vigilante for Jesus.

My saga began one evening while watching the six o'clock news: violence, violence. *Was the entire city under attack by swarms of home-grown terrorists?* These offenders behaved as though they were depraved demons. *How could they shoot people as if they were playing a violent video game?*

As I viewed the unwarranted violence, Jesus spoke to me, saying He was going to empower me with supernatural abilities to stop crimes while they were being committed. My superpowers encompassed running faster than a speeding car and deflecting bullets and other deadly weapons aimed at harming me. After stopping a crime in progress, I was to deliver the gospel message to both perpetrator and victim. I would feel my face emitting heat, and everyone who looked at me would see my face glowing. I would never know whether the offenders or victims would accept the free gift of salvation. No one would be able to describe me after an encounter. Witnesses would give different descriptions.

Jesus said He would cause me to be invisible in some instances where I would stand next to someone, and they would not recognize me. *How cool is that?* The Lord Jesus told me that I would be directed to where a crime was being committed, and I would interrupt it immediately.

Unfortunately, large urban cities in the United States have become meccas for lawlessness. In the twenty-fourth chapter of Matthew, the Lord tells us that "because iniquity shall abound, the love of many will wax cold." In II Thessalonians, second chapter, we are told that "the secret power of lawlessness is already at work."

The Lord Jesus explained that I would not be able to eliminate all crime in my city. Still, my interventions would save hundreds of lives, physically and spiritually. Many people would think about changing their sinful lifestyles and pursuing salvation in the name of Jesus. I enthusiastically accepted my quest to become the Vigilante for Jesus!

DRIVE-BY SHOOTER

One Saturday morning, I decided to go downtown on Michigan Avenue to shop for new shoes and dress shirts to wear to church. Although I have a Nissan Rogue, I prefer riding on public transportation when I go shopping downtown because the bus stops in front of the condominium building where I live; also, traffic is horrific, and parking is too expensive.

Walking down the walkway from my building to Lake Shore Drive, I noticed an expensive Mercedes SUV being driven very slowly. The windows were darkly tinted, and the rear driver's side window was being lowered, although it was quite chilly outside. I felt a strange sensation; all of my senses were on overdrive. I knew a crime was about to be committed, and I knew I had to intervene.

I saw a lady holding her little daughter's hand as they walked toward the bus stop. The shooter was going to spray them with bullets from an automatic weapon, which was now visible. My eyesight became keener, and my legs seemed stronger and more powerful. I ran faster than humanly possible. I pushed the lady and her child to the ground as gently as I could. They were startled and started screaming and attempted to fight me until they heard the barrage of bullets coming from the SUV. When the bullets bounced off my body, we were all surprised. A protective shield enveloped me and expanded to cover the lady and her child. Shell casings littered the sidewalk as the vehicle sped away. All three of us emerged unscathed. The covering mysteriously disappeared. Jesus had covered us with an invisible cloak.

When the two other victims stood up, they could not stop thanking me for saving their lives. Quickly, I corrected them, telling them that Jesus had saved all of us by activating the shield. I began telling her all about Jesus and how much He loved her and her child. She told me she was so lonely and downtrodden because her husband had been killed in Afghanistan during the troop withdrawal. She was devastated and disillusioned because she felt God had abandoned them by allowing her husband to be killed. She and her daughter cried themselves to sleep every night. I told her how God sent His Son Jesus to die for her and everyone. I told her that God supernaturally preserved her life because of His love for her.

Furthermore, Jesus sent me to help rescue her and her child. I explained that this was my first time being a vigilante for Jesus and that I felt awesome. I had found my purpose for life. I told her that she should pray and ask Jesus to show her His purpose for her life. She tearfully agreed that she would begin seeking Jesus.

By this time, a large crowd had gathered around us, and people began questioning the lady, but not me. Although I was standing right there, everyone began looking for me. The police arrived and started questioning the crowd of spectators and the victims. Although everyone looked for me, no one saw me. When the police asked for my description, everyone gave conflicting reports; some people said I was short. Some people said I was African American, while others said I was a tall Hispanic or Caucasian. *What?* Being a superhero was so much fun. The police placed markers by each shell casing; there were at least fifty.

Only one phase of my assignment was complete; I had to find the perpetrators and give them the gospel message. Remember, I am the vigilante for Jesus. Whether I flew or ran exceptionally fast, I caught up with the criminals about ten blocks away, where they had stopped for a red light. I positioned myself directly in front of their car. They looked terrified as I ordered them out of their SUV. I felt my face emanating heat. They stood on the sidewalk and averted their eyes as I talked to them. They asked if I could not look directly at them because my shining face was scary. I told them that Jesus sent me to prevent them from murdering an innocent person and her small child.

They started confessing all of their criminal activities to me. "Well, see, we were high, and we stole the Mercedes from a rival gang member, not knowing he had a cache of weapons in the trunk. We decided to kill someone while driving their car and then ditch the car so it could be traced back to them. They would be so busy running from the police they would stop searching for us. We have been carjacking and doing drive-by shootings for about a year. We have shot over fifty people and robbed several businesses. We never expected to see bullets ricochet off a person and for that person to pursue us on foot and overtake us with his glowing face. Are you going to kill us and send us to Hell? Who are you or what are you?"

First, I cannot determine whether you go to Hell or Heaven, and I cannot forgive your sins, but I know someone who can. His name is Jesus; I am merely His servant, his vigilante. My mission is to stop crimes while they are being committed and give both victims and criminals the gospel message. God sent His Son Jesus to be born of a virgin, to be crucified on a Roman cross for everyone's sins so we could live forever with Him in Heaven. All we have to do is to accept Him as our Lord and Savior. We must first sincerely repent of our sins. Pretending to repent is futile because God knows what is in your heart. I explained that being a Christian had benefits, as stated in Psalm 103. David wrote that Jesus would forgive all of your sins, heal all your diseases, and crown you with tender mercies and loving-kindness. He will also redeem your life from destruction. I explained to them that they would probably go to prison, but Jesus was able to sustain them anywhere. As they returned to their auto, they thanked me for telling them about Jesus.

I do not know what happened to them; however, I saw several police cars speeding in their direction with sirens blaring.

2

SHOPPING

After attending church, I went home to change into casual clothing to walk around the Rush Street area. I never buy anything in that vicinity because the prices are too exorbitant for me, but it is enjoyable to window shop in the high-end stores. While strolling by an exclusive jewelry store on Huron Street, I noticed a sports car parked in front of the store in a no-parking zone. The driver looked really nervous, which piqued my curiosity. After looking through the jewelry store window, I glimpsed a man holding a gun and talking to several employees. I looked closer and saw that the robber was carrying a large bag in one hand and his weapon in the other hand. Immediately, I knew what I had to do. Although you had to be buzzed in, I walked into the store. I could see why the gunman was granted access; he was dressed to impress.

When I walked into the store, I told the robber to place his gun on the floor and leave the bag on the counter. God told me the man's name was Matthew. He slowly turned around to see where the voice was coming from. After looking at my glowing face, he placed the revolver on the floor and handed the bag to an employee.

He attempted to talk to me without looking directly at me. "I need these items because I want things I could never afford, no matter how many jobs I had. What difference does it make? The store has insurance. They won't lose a penny. I want to feel important and be admired by my relatives and friends. Who are you anyway, and why is your face shining? I'm nice, but my partner in the car out front is ruthless; he is a murderer. You had better let me leave with the jewelry before he comes in and kills everyone."

The employee said, "He would have to be buzzed in, and we are not going to allow him entry. I have already notified the police."

As soon as Matthew finished speaking, God also revealed that the name of his partner in crime was Nate.

Nate walked in. I suppose I caused the lock to malfunction when I just walked in. Nate walked in with an assault rifle in his hand and immediately asked who the hell I was with my glowing face. I calmly replied VJ, Vigilante for Jesus. Nate said he didn't care who I was with my freaky face because I would die in a few minutes. Before I could warn Nate and tell him what happened to people who tried to harm me, he pulled the trigger several times, aiming for my head. My invisible shield caused the bullets to ricochet, striking Nate in the exact places he aimed at me. He fell to the floor dead. I was sorry I had not been able to warn Nate.

Everyone in the store started screaming, especially Matthew. After they all calmed down, I delivered the gospel message to all of them, and I ended with an invitation to follow Jesus and repeat the sinner's prayer. 'Dear Lord Jesus, I know I am a sinner, and I am so sorry. Please forgive me. I believe you came to earth, born of a virgin, and that you died for my sins; I sincerely repent. I believe that you were crucified and rose again on the third day and are alive today, seated at the right hand of God the Father. Please live in me and be the Lord of my life.'

Everyone repeated the sinner's prayer; however, I don't know if they were sincere. A few minutes later, I heard sirens and a voice over a loudspeaker. One of the employees gestured to the police, telling them it was okay for them to enter. I walked out of the front door. There was a crowd on the sidewalk and a tremendous police presence. No one noticed me as I walked out of the jewelry shop. I mingled with the crowd and listened to the employees, and Matthew's explanation of what had happened. An ambulance arrived shortly and brought out Nate's body.

Reporters arrived after the police had attempted to find out the details of the robbery. Whenever anyone tried to describe me, their stories were inconsistent. "I mean, he was tall, not average height. No, he was short. He was Latino. No, he was definitely African American." It went on and on. Matthew kept saying, "I'm sorry, Mr. V J. Tell Jesus that I am truly sorry for everything I have done wrong."

On the 10 p.m. news, they talked about a man who called himself V.J., a vigilante for Jesus. Was this a new superhero who could not be killed? Had Jesus himself sent V.J. to stop all the crime in our city? One reporter actually said everyone should pray to the Christian deity, Jesus, to continue allowing V.J. to thwart the crime in our city.

3

GANG RECRUITMENT

One Saturday, I took public transportation to an area of the city where I had no reason to venture. I was on Eighteenth and Leavitt, walking down an alley at about six o'clock in the evening. I had no idea what I would encounter and why the Lord Jesus wanted me here. I heard blood-curdling screaming and pleas for God's help and mercy. After opening a garage door where the noise was emanating, I saw a young teenage boy on his knees begging a gang leader not to sexually violate his thirteen-year-old sister.

The teenage boy explained that he was a Christian, a choir member, and leader of the Youth for Christ Ministry. The gang leader was unsympathetic. He told Pedro that if he refused to join the gang, his sister would be violated by all ten of them and that every time Pedro refused to obey a command, she would be attacked again by all of them.

I walked in boldly and told them to untie the girl, allow Pedro to leave, and that they would never attempt to recruit Pedro again. All ten of them laughed at me until they were bent over. One gang member pulled out his switchblade, and another one picked up a sledgehammer and ran toward me. At first, the rest of them just watched me as my face began to pulsate. I knew my face was glowing. One gang member said, "Hell no, I'm not about to fight this supernatural freak." He walked out.

I warned all of them that trying to hurt me would have tragic repercussions. As the Vigilante for Jesus, I was protected by Jesus; whatever they attempted to do to me would happen to them. I told them that Jesus wanted none of them to perish but to live eternally with Him. I assumed they had a Catholic background because of their ethnicity and neighborhood. They had been taught about Jesus their whole life. I explained that Jesus was offering them a second chance for redemption.

They looked confused. I instructed Pedro to take his sister and go home. The sadistic gang leader told Pedro not to leave and not to go near his sister. Pedro heeded my instructions, and he and his sister ran from the garage. Everything seemed to happen in slow motion. All gang members were armed with guns, sledgehammers, baseball bats, and knives. They all rushed toward me at once. Their knives cut them, the sledgehammers beat them, the bats hit them, and the bullets shot them. It was surreal, like a dance recital, only a brutal, deadly one. Only one person had escaped.

When I looked toward the garage door, I saw Pedro and his little sister standing there with a look of horror on their faces. I told them that God honored Pedro's commitment and resolve to follow Jesus regardless of the consequences. When Pedro finished crying, he told me he felt like Daniel and his three friends when they refused to compromise their religious values by bowing to King Nebuchadnezzar's statue.

Pedro and his family were safe, and the entire neighborhood was safe from this brutal street gang; however, I was saddened by the death of nine souls who had no chance of redemption. Although ambulances were called immediately, no one survived. Hopefully, the one gang member who left will repent and be saved.

4

CAR JACKING

The Lord led me to the Bridgeport area in Chicago near Thirty First Street. I drove my SUV to a quiet neighborhood at seven thirty in the evening. I parked across the street from a car inhabited by four teenagers. *Were they waiting for someone to come out of the house?* About ten minutes later, a middle-aged gentleman drove out of his garage in a new Lexus. Instinctively, I knew they were going to attempt to carjack him. I prayed to God and asked Him to show extreme mercy to the criminals if they attempted to hurt me when I intervened.

As I suspected, the teens took off following the Lexus. When the person driving the Lexus stopped at a traffic light, the teenagers stopped directly behind him and exited their car with guns drawn. After surrounding his car, the man raised his hands and got out of the car. He was much older than I thought initially. Sobbing and shaking, he held out the keys to his car.

I exited my car, walked up to the man, and reassured him everything would be fine. Shock and awe ensued as the criminals turned their weapons on me. My face began pulsating; apparently, it looked scarier than at other times because all the hoodlums dropped their guns and stood with their hands in the air.

They asked what I was going to do with them. Before I could answer, the police arrived and arrested the gang of car thieves. I stayed on the scene and began witnessing to the police. I told them that Jesus sent me to stop the carjacking because he loves this old man, the carjackers, and them. I told the police officers that they needed Jesus every hour, every minute, especially because of the harrowing nature of their job. There were four of them left at the scene. The old man said he thanked Jesus for sending me to his rescue. I asked the police officers if they would like to make Jesus the Lord of their life. I was shocked when they all said yes and repeated the Sinner's Prayer after me. *Just imagine if all police officers were saved.* As usual, I just got into my car and drove home.

The police officers looked around to see where I had gone, but they could not locate me, nor could they describe me to their superiors. A neighbor came out of his house and told the police that he had witnessed everything and knew I was the Vigilante for Jesus. V.J. was gaining notoriety all over the city. Police were warning criminals that they had better stop their illegal activities because they never knew when the Vigilante for Jesus would appear and that V.J. was a force to be reckoned with. The best thing that happened that day was that on the ten o'clock news, I heard that church attendance was increasing, and that people were beginning to believe in Jesus more and more. People were thanking Jesus for preventing some of the crimes in their city. I am so happy that Jesus chose me to be the Vigilante for Jesus.

5

KIDNAPPER

One sunny day, I was led to a park where several children were playing. As I surveyed the area, I noticed a middle-aged man talking to a boy who looked to be about six years old. Apparently, the boy's parents had not told him about stranger danger. The man held a puppy in his hands, attempting to entice the boy to get into his car to play with the puppy. The young child was about to enter the car when I stood between them. They were both shocked to see me.

Several women were close by having a heated conversation. I told the boy to go to his mother.

The parents were not being vigilant, allowing the kidnapper/pedophile to exploit their distraction. I felt my face getting hot as I talked to the would-be abductor. I told him that I knew his name was Jack and that he had a criminal record as a sex offender. When children were present, he was not supposed to be within five hundred feet of a playground or elementary school.

He looked at my glowing face, unafraid or even curious. He had an insolent smirk on his face. That reaction to my appearance had never happened before. After telling me to mind my own business, he jumped into his car and took off with wheels screeching loudly. The noise caused the parents to look around and run toward the little boy. After the little child told the parents what happened, they screamed and ran to me, telling me how much they appreciated my intervention. This was my golden opportunity to tell them about Jesus.

I explained to them that Jesus loved them so much that He led me there to rescue their son from what would have been a horrific experience. I asked if any of them were Christians. They all said no, but they wanted to know about Jesus and how He knew what was about to happen. I found out that none of them had a Bible or attended church. Some of their parents had been Christians, but they never embraced any religion. Most of them thought Christians were all phony. They now believed in a higher power who wanted to embrace and protect them.

I explained the gospel by reciting First Corinthians fifteen, one through six, where the Apostle Paul wrote that Jesus died for their sins, was buried, and raised on the third day, and appeared to many after His resurrection. I told them they must sincerely repent and ask

Jesus to be the Lord of their life. They unanimously agreed. I explained to them that I had to leave to prevent another child from being kidnapped.

A family reunion was taking place in the location I arrived at next. Jack had just kidnapped a young boy and was driving away as six people were running after his car. They were not fast enough to catch him. I sped up and got to the intersection before Jack. As I exited my auto, Jack sped up instead of stopping and attempted to run over me. His car hit my protective shield and sustained front-end damage. Neither Jack nor the child were hurt.

I ordered Jack out of the vehicle; he had to obey because the Lord had given me that ability. I told him that his heinous crime spree had ended and that he had an opportunity to ask for forgiveness, sincerely repent, and ask Jesus to be the Lord of his life. He looked at my glowing face and said, "No thanks." That smirk was still on his face when the police arrived. God directed me to look at him intensely in his eyes. Wow! I don't know what he saw, but that smirk was replaced with a look of fear and dread.

After Jack was taken away, the police and the families of the boy surrounded me, asking a million questions. I simply told them to thank Jesus for rescuing their child. I told them all about Jesus and why they should worship Him not only for this rescue but also for dying for their sins and enabling them to live with Him eternally. They listened intently, and the few Christians there nodded their heads in agreement. The rest of them were deep in thought.

I do not know how many of them accepted the free gift of salvation; however, they thought about it. I was surprised when a policeman said, amen.

I never knew what Jack saw when he looked into my eyes. Perhaps he saw himself being sexually violated frequently in prison, or maybe he saw himself suffering eternally in Hell.

6

CTA ROBBERIES

One evening I was led to take the CTA Red Line train from 95th Street to Cermak Road. The train was relatively quiet until it stopped at Seventy-Ninth Street, where five teenagers/young adults boarded. Their long coats did not entirely conceal the weapons they were carrying. They surveyed and assessed the entire car. Two of them stationed themselves in the rear, two in the front, and one in the middle of the train car.

Although there were several empty seats, no one sat down. After announcing a robbery, the person in the middle of the train pulled a large garbage bag from inside his coat and instructed everyone to place their belongings in the bag. The other four robbers brandished their guns. The criminal with the bag began collecting mobile devices, wallets, and jewelry from the passengers.

I walked to the rear of the train and told the two robbers to give me their guns. After looking at my glowing face, they complied. Humiliated and afraid, they sat down. I snatched the bag from the middle terrorist and returned the belongings to the passengers. I carefully placed the weapons in the bag. By this time, the two criminals in the front of the train were so terrified they brought me their guns and put them in the bag, and then I started preaching to my captive audience.

"Everyone, my name is V.J., and I am the Vigilante for Jesus." One of the robbers jumped up at this announcement and said he knew it. "These people who attempted to rob you are sinners, but we are all sinners. In Romans three, verses twenty-three and twenty-four, we are told that all have sinned and fallen short of the glory of God, being justified freely by His grace through the redemption that is in Christ Jesus. All you have to do is sincerely repent and ask Jesus to be the Lord of your life. If you are not sincere, Jesus will know it because He knows what is in your heart. Now is the time. There might not ever be another time for redemption. The scriptures tell us to call upon Him while He is near."

I delivered the gospel message and led as many as were willing in the Sinner's Prayer. I gave them my personal testimony about my abusive parents and how I wanted to murder them while they slept. Jesus sent my distant cousin Susan to rescue me by paying my parents to allow me to live with her. She was a real Christian who took me to church, read the Bible daily, and prayed unceasingly. Her exemplary character caused me to want Jesus to be my Savior and for Him to use me to further His kingdom.

He has granted my wish by allowing me to be His vigilante. I related to them all that had happened so far. I explained how joyful and fulfilled my life has been since Jesus came into my heart. There was not a dry eye in that train car when it stopped. The robbers got off with me and shook my hand. I do not know what happened to them, but I pray they ended their life of crime and accepted the free gift of salvation.

7

SWARM

On a warm Sunday evening, I decided I wanted a Slurpee. I drove to the closest convenience store and placed my order. There were two cashiers on duty and no other customers. After paying for my drink, I was about to pick up my cup and leave when I heard screeching tire sounds and shattering glass. Twenty-four teens entered the store after exiting six cars parked in front of the store.

Their age range was from fifteen to nineteen. "Crash and grab" is the term used these days for the criminal action I was watching.

They had driven one of the cars into the door of the store. It wasn't after hours when the store would have been closed. Laughing and screaming were all I heard from them. They smashed shelves and stole everything they could get their hands on. They had large carpenter's bags, which they filled quickly with merchandise. I had a feeling this wasn't their first rodeo.

At first, the cashiers and I were mesmerized. After I was able to snap out of my paralytic state of shock and realize I was here to thwart a swarm robbery, I knew exactly what I had to do. I took my stance at the front of the door where the auto's front end was lodged. With a loud voice and vibrating face, I ordered the swarm to look at me. There was a hushed silence as they stopped looting and turned toward me. Fortunately for them, no one had weapons. I ordered them to take every item from the bags and place them on the shelves that were not destroyed. They did exactly as I had ordered. Some shelves were too severely damaged to be repaired. Even the refrigerator doors were broken. I knew they would obey because Jesus told me they had to obey me.

I began addressing the swarm by telling them they had no direction or sense of right and wrong. Jesus had already told me they were unchurched. I asked if any of them had heard of Jesus. All of them said they had because of Christmas and all the festivities associated with the holiday. I asked if any of them believed that Jesus was the Savior of the whole world. No one said anything. I gave them the gospel message from I Corinthians 15: 1-4.

I explained that they could all be forgiven of all their sins if they would sincerely repent and accept Jesus as their Lord and Savior. I asked them if they realized that retail theft had a spiral effect. They all shook their heads and murmured, "No." Theft increased prices for everyone, including their parents, siblings, friends, and the poor and needy.

I explained that if they continued their life of crime, some of them would be incarcerated or even killed. I frightened them when I told them that I was going to talk to each of their parents about Jesus and about the criminal activities in which their children were engaged. I also talked to the two clerks and extended an invitation to all of them to repeat the Sinner's Prayer.

When the police arrived, they impounded all the vehicles, including the one they had to call a tow truck to extricate from the front window. I followed the paddy wagon to the police station and talked to each parent about their child and, most importantly, Jesus.

As usual, no one could describe me, not even the police. I watched the entire incident on the news that night. The newscast ended with the excellent news that church attendance had doubled since VJ had become the Vigilante for Jesus. Crime had not decreased significantly yet.

8

CAR DEALERSHIP THEFT

The Lord Jesus told me to get dressed and drive my car to a closed suburban car dealership. I had just gone to bed; it was eleven o'clock at night. After parking my car and turning off my headlights, I waited to see what would happen. After five minutes, I saw people in two SUVs exit their cars, and peer through the windows of the dealerships' garage.

The thieves tried jimmying the door of the garage to no avail. Finally, one of the thieves threw a brick through the small top window of the garage. They boosted a smaller person up to the window, and he climbed through the opening. Once inside, the smaller person opened the door, and they all entered. I wondered how they were going to steal cars without keys. Even with keyless entry, you had to have keys nearby.

I heard cars starting, and I saw the big door of the garage opening. I recalled reading that by using an amplifier and a relay one could trick the car's computer system into believing the keys were near. The autos would be unlocked, and the thieves could just drive away because the code was broken. I got out of my car and stood at the garage door entrance.

Altogether, there were nine car thieves. When the first driver saw me, he put his car in park and managed to stop the vehicle before it hit me. Knowing they had to obey me, I ordered them to turn off the cars and get out. They looked like zombies. Some of them were armed, and one person shot at me before I had time to warn him of the consequences.

The bullet ricocheted and shot him in the heart, killing him instantly. They all wanted to run, but they could not. There was crying, moaning, cursing, and praying. Two of them asked who I was and if they could approach me. After giving them permission to come close to me, they stared at my shining face, more curious than frightened. I asked to whom they were praying. They said God, of course. I took full advantage of this opportunity.

I explained that Jesus had always existed and that He was one part of the Trinity: Father, Son, Holy Spirit. I told them that Jesus came to earth and died for the sins of everyone so that those who chose Him as Lord and Savior could live with him forever in heaven. I had to tell them about the original sin caused by Adam and Eve's disobedience and how Jesus was born of a virgin, impregnated by the Holy Spirit.

I explained that Jesus never sinned, but He was crucified for our sins and that He was resurrected from the grave after three days. I was astounded to know they had never heard this before. Two of them wept and asked what they had to do to be saved. Their names were Ron and Charlie. They shed tears of remorse and repeated the Sinner's Prayer after me. The rest of them just stood there looking confused.

The silent alarm had been triggered; the police surrounded the building. Ron and Charlie stood there with me while the rest of the gang ran from the ensuing police. I didn't have to say a word because the police knew I had prevented another crime. Eventually, all of them were apprehended and faced criminal charges. It saddened me that one person had to die, but I was overjoyed that two people repented and asked Jesus to become the Lord of their lives.

Church attendance kept increasing, and more Bibles were being purchased. Although crime was only diminishing a little, it was a start. I know that lawlessness will increase more and more, but I am thankful that through Jesus, some crimes have been prevented, and some people have become Christians.

9

SHOPPING CENTER FLASH MOB

One Saturday morning, the Lord told me to go to one of the largest upscale shopping centers in the state. I assumed someone was going to burglarize a store or attempt to carjack someone in the parking lot. Walking into Nordstrom, I noticed everything was reduced drastically because of the end-of-season reductions. That is the only time I would be able to purchase items from there.

I did not know what to expect, so I walked around to each department. No one acted suspiciously, and there was no evidence of a robbery. Suddenly, about fifty people converged on the first floor, armed and wild. They were screaming, and the security guard was shot. *How could this escalate so quickly?* They pulled out those carpenter bags. *Again?* They disseminated to three areas of the store: designer handbags, authentic jewelry, and designer shoes. Overwhelmed by the swiftness and precision targets of the criminals, the salespeople moved aside with their hands over their mouths.

God told me to wait until the mob left the store. God told me that He would tell me each robber's name and location and that I would track them down within hours and recover all of the stolen merchandise.

I calmly walked to the parking lot and stood in front of one of the cars where four perpetrators were about to leave. I ordered all four of them to exit the car, knowing they had to obey me. Apparently, my face was glowing because they looked terrified and begged me not to kill them. I told them I had no intention to kill them, but on the contrary, I offered them life instead of death through belief in Jesus Christ.

After delivering the gospel message to them, none of them wanted to repeat the Sinner's Prayer. Their hearts were hardened already at such young ages. The police arrived in full force and saw all the weapons on the ground and the auto-filled with merchandise. Most law enforcement knew me or knew about me. They arrested the criminals and nodded their approval to me. They knew better than to question me or ask witnesses about me. I simply walked away.

After a police chase, two carloads of criminals exited their cars, broke into a nearby residence, and held five people hostage. Three young men and two young women were held hostage by four criminals holding guns to their heads and threatening to shoot them if the police intervened.

I calmly walked up to the house while the police called SWAT. After entering the locked door, I saw everyone seated in a beautiful, spacious living room. I believe they were all college students sharing the expenses of the house. Five weapons were all pointing at me. I prayed to Jesus not to let anyone attempt to shoot me. I did not want to see anyone killed today. My face was glowing as I talked to the gangsters, telling them what would happen if they attempted to shoot me. They believed me because they knew what had happened to people who attempted to harm me. Apparently, they watched the news or read it on their cell phones.

Although they dropped their weapons, I did not give the all-clear to the police until I delivered the gospel message. I told them and the hostages how Jesus died for everyone because all have sinned and come short of the glory of God. One of the criminals asked me why God would send Jesus to die for us. I told him because He loves us that much. He said he did not understand. I told him and all the others to pray to Jesus and ask for forgiveness of their sins, to sincerely repent and realize what Jesus has done for them this day.

The people being held hostage were Christians and began praising God and singing and sharing their faith with the offenders. Most of them started crying and asking for forgiveness and mercy. They were on their knees praying when the police rushed in. Even the police were astounded.

After the criminals were arrested, they told the police where the rest of their gang could be located. All flash mob members were arrested within hours, and all merchandise was returned. I do not know what happened to the rest of the mob, but no one was shot. I praised

Jesus for the few young hoodlums who sincerely repented and gave their lives to Jesus.

Church attendance kept increasing, and crime kept diminishing. I realized that my efforts were only a drop in the bucket; however, I am so privileged to be the Vigilante for Jesus.

10

BULLY DOWN

After attending church, I headed home to spend a leisurely day reading and studying Bible scriptures; however, I was led to take the Red Line train to Chinatown. I knew I had to stop a crime that was being committed. When I exited the train, I saw an elderly Chinese lady walking down Twenty-Second Street. She had a large cross around her neck and a Bible in her hand.

Noticing a large man rushing toward her, I ran and stood in front of her. I do not know what nationality he was: Hispanic, African American, Italian. He had an accent when he spoke, but I could not identify it. He told me to get out of the way because he had to knock the lady down and kill her by banging her head onto the sidewalk. Before I could warn him not to strike me, he attempted to punch me with such rage that he broke both wrists and several bones in his hands. Howling with pain, he told me that he would kill me later. I gave my attention to the lady standing behind me. She told me that she knew who I was and thanked Jesus every day for me. I hugged her and kissed her tiny hand as she cried tears of joy.

I quickly caught up with the Chinatown bully. The Lord revealed to me that he had caused a Chinese man to have permanent brain damage after beating him mercilessly earlier that day. Although the Bully's hands had several broken bones and his wrists were broken, he attempted to accost two men who were exiting a nearby building. These men were small in stature, but much younger than the Bully. To my surprise, he attempted to butt their heads together. I was delayed getting to the two men to save them. When I reached them, the two men had the Bully on the ground in a fatal headlock.

Although Bully was about six feet, two inches tall, and weighed about two hundred sixty pounds, he was no match for these two. They were each about five feet four inches in height and weighed about one hundred fifty pounds. I prevented Bully's death by persuading the two men that Jesus did not want them to become murderers.

They listened attentively as I delivered the gospel message to all of them. They had caused irreparable damage to Bully's body already: broken ribs, kidney damage, broken femur, and broken kneecaps. Glancing around the neighborhood, I saw the building where the two men had emerged from: Karate Training Academy. They were the instructors. I told them they would never have anything to fear from the Bully again because he would always be in a wheelchair while locked up in jail. The Bully wanted nothing to do with Jesus. He cursed me and the name of Jesus. All I could do was pray for him.

I have been the Vigilante for Jesus for ten years, and hundreds of crimes have been thwarted. Our city's church attendance is at an all-time high, although crimes have not ceased exponentially. Jesus told me that these were the last days and lawlessness would increase, but His church would be raptured before the tribulation. It is our duty to spread the gospel message to as many people who will listen. His desire is that none should perish, but all should accept the free gift of salvation.

ABOUT THE AUTHOR

Katherine Michelle Woods is a retired elementary educator who believes faith in God can transform troubled lives. As society becomes more technologically advanced, belief in God dwindles. Therefore, Ms. Woods is committed to publishing books highlighting that God is still in the miracle-working business.

Katherine Michelle Woods has written and published four books. Her first book is **All Children are Mine**; the second book is **Rescued, Redeemed, Raptured**; the third book is **Love Jesus**; and the fourth book is **Vigilante for Jesus**.

9 798330 470815